HISTORIC
SITES *of*
CANADA

Right: ***Baie de Gaspé, Québec.***
Master-navigator and explorer
Jacques Cartier of St. Malo landed
here on 24 July 1534, raising a wooden
cross which bore the arms of France
and the inscription "Vivre le Roi de
France" before sailing home again.
The implication seems to have been
clear enough to Huron Indian chief
Donnacona, who conveyed by signs
that this was his country and nobody
should erect a cross without his
permission; but he allowed Cartier to
leave with two of his teenage sons,
who were to be shown to the French
king.

A year later, Cartier was edging his
way upriver to the Iroquois villages of
Stadocona (present-day Québec)
where he returned the two boys to
their father, and Hochelaga
(Montréal). This time he went back to
France believing that he had found
gold (iron pyrites) and diamonds
(quartz). Was it the end of the
beginning of the beginning or the end?

HISTORIC SITES *of* CANADA

BRERETON GREENHOUS

PHOTOGRAPHY BY
WINSTON FRASER

Bramley Books

Text and Captions
Brereton Greenhous

Photography
Winston Fraser

Design
Jill Coote

Commissioning
Andrew Preston
Edward Doling
Laura Potts

Editorial
Gill Waugh

Production
Ruth Arthur
David Proffit
Sally Connolly
Andrew Whitelaw

Director of Production
Gerald Hughes

CLB 2571
© 1991 Colour Library Books Ltd,
Godalming, Surrey, England.
All rights reserved.
This edition published 1991 by
Bramley Books.
Printed and bound in Singapore.
ISBN 0 86283 898 3

Right: **Confederation Chamber, Charlottetown, Prince Edward Island**.
It might be argued that Canada as a nation was conceived here in September 1864. The deed was done in the course of a conference belatedly arranged by the governments of Nova Scotia, New Brunswick and Prince Edward Island, at the anxious wish of French and English delegates from Canada East (Québec) and West (Ontario). Why Charlottetown? Because reluctant Prince Edward Island politicians declined to participate unless it was held there; even so, the Islanders rejected Confederation until 1873. Newfoundlanders resisted for much longer.

Driven by British pressure to become self-supporting and self-defending, by their own fears of the republican ogres to the south and by French Canadian ambitions to re-establish Québec as a separate province, the conclusions reached there were only acceptable to some delegates as the least undesirable among several unpleasant alternatives. In the end, the only true Fathers of Confederation were the representatives from Nova Scotia, who certainly did not represent the public opinion of their colony, New Brunswick and Canada.

CONTENTS

*I*NTRODUCTION

*T*his book is filled with pictures of historic artifacts – which is the technical term for what my dictionary defines as 'the material end-products of human thought and effort.' You and I would more likely call them old things.

Most of these particular old things are buildings of one kind or another. Large ones and small ones, beautiful ones and ugly ones, wooden, brick and stone ones – they are all historic artifacts. So are gravestones and locomotives, firehalls and statues, airplanes and steel rails, threshing machines, clocks, bridges, lighthouses and mine tailings.

Although history is really about ideas and concepts, not things, it is most readily understood (because most of us comprehend the concrete better than the abstract) through the study of artifacts. They tell us, for example, what raw materials were most readily available to our forebears at a particular place and time, and which could most easily be worked with the tools of that day. Conversely, we can learn something about the nature and capabilities of the tools themselves from the things they were used to produce.

That, in turn, offers a good measure of the complexity and intricacies of the society which used them. The more specialized and complicated a tool is, the more sophisticated and multi-faceted the culture that devised it will probably prove to be. Three centuries ago, for example, these words might have been written with a goose quill pen; two centuries ago, with a steel-nib; one century ago, with a typewriter perhaps, or at least a fountain pen; and today with a personal computer, word-processing software and a laser printer.

Getting back to buildings: where they stand or once stood, together with their contents (or simply even their rubble) and their various relationships to each other, tell us much about the habits, needs, ambitions and desires of the communities responsible for raising them. Forts, whether merely stockaded rectangles or bastion, ravelin and scarp of fitted masonry, once secured borders or key communications centres, majestically (but often vainly) trying to assert territorial and economic prerogatives, like Louisbourg's brooding bastions, or merely labelling company property, like Fort Carlton's rotting palisades.

Cities and towns speak to us of production and trade, of growth or decay. Georgian public architecture paradoxically recalls Victorian values, while Baroque equates with opulence. Crude construction hints at poverty. Ornate shrines and simple chapels proclaim the religious tenets more than the financial status of those who paid for them. Schools and universities suggest a thirst for knowledge, canals and railways record a demand for bulk transportation of heavy goods.

None of these things existed in North American before the white man came, however. Although the social and political organization of the aboriginal inhabitants was complex, they had no written language, no accurate record of the past, and thus no institutional path to technological learning. They had tamed fire but never learned to smelt metal – those blessed with open lodes of copper ore treated it simply as malleable stone. They had not yet conceived the wheel, and knew nothing of crop rotation. Their tools were primitive, their technological triumphs no greater than the birchbark canoe and the bone-ribbed, skin-covered kayak and umiak.

The first Europeans to arrive, almost a thousand years ago, were little more advanced than the natives they encountered, although they knew the written word (even if few of them could use it), had mastered the wheel, and could forge iron. They came intermittently, in tentative explorations over two or three hundred years, in open, rudderless boats, finding their way by the sun and stars, and the *fauna* and *detritus* of the sea, wielding swords and axes, building sod huts and perhaps timbered halls. Each time they came, they tarried only a little while – a year or two, at most – and then they sailed away, leaving only the barest traces of their passing.

Their successors, navigating by compass and astrolabe and dead-reckoning in decked and portly square-rigged ships, came – this time to stay – in the early sixteenth century. Fishermen and explorers first, then missionaries, farmers and artisans, and they brought the plough and the musket with them. Glass, books, stonemasonry, horses and cattle, techniques of tillage and crop rotation, and the hard-learned knowledge of a thousand other things.

French power declined and British power rose, enforced from the muzzles of cannon, exercised by expatriate aristocrats and clergymen at first, then by farmers and shopkeepers. A marginal economy became a stable one, a French colony became British, and a century later, three of the six British North American colonies (the larger part of the present-day Canada was still the exclusive trading preserve of the Governor and Company of Adventurers of England Trading into Hudson's Bay) anxiously confederated themselves into the Dominion of Canada.

Judicious bribery and wholesome self-interest soon stretched their dominion *a mari usque ad mare*. Urbane politicians, buoyant capitalists and smug engineers inflicted steamboats and railways on us, telegraphs and telephones, stock exchanges, oil wells and automobiles. Niagara's awesome falls were harnessed to light Windsor homes and power Toronto streetcars. Suddenly one

summer, Dawson City – shanty town incarnate! – was created by a gold rush to the land of the midnight sun; flumes became dredges, dredges became mines, and Dawson collapsed into ghost town status almost as suddenly as it had risen to boom town.

Industrialization, urbanization, quickened the pace of change through the turn of the nineteenth century. Two world wars, income tax, women's suffrage, and the miasma of a Great Depression brought us department stores and cinemas, the Montreal Forum and Maple Leaf Gardens, polyester and Pablum and paint rollers. Halifax exploded, insulin was discovered, and uranium mined; cars proliferated, radio and television were invented, air travel became a commonplace and the St. Lawrence Seaway bore ocean-going ships past Thunder Bay.

History has both a beginning and an end for a historian of the author's conservative, perhaps pedantic, turn of mind. Because history is founded in the written record, it only begins with mastery of the written word. Before that in time lie the unholy realms of archaeology and cultural anthropology, rooted in myth and legend and speculative, if logical, deduction. Artifacts in plenty, but not historic artifacts.

At the other end of my time-line, history demands a perspective which only a substantial interval can bring. More recent events are better categorized as news or current affairs. They, too, have their artifacts – millions of them! – but they are not historic, either. Not yet. One day, God help us, they will be.

Thus none of the historic sites and artifacts portrayed in these

Above: **Parliament Buildings, Ottawa, Ontario.**
After much debate by the colonial representatives (and little by the Parliament of Westminster) the British North America Act was signed into law by Queen Victoria on 29 March 1867. It was proclaimed here on 1 July 1867, the date which is now celebrated as Canada's birthday.

The BNA Act in an appropriately contemporary form was eventually 'patriated', and became an exclusively Canadian affair as the Constitution Act on 17 April 1982 at a rain-lashed ceremony on Parliament Hill; but it was a tainted triumph for prime minister Pierre Elliot Trudeau. Québec, thwarted in its desire to be a "distinct society" and hold a veto over any amending formula, failed to sign the constitutional accord supporting the Act.

pages relate to events that occurred more than a thousand years ago, or less than thirty; and all but one of them fall within the last six hundred years, most within the last three hundred. Regrettably – but perhaps inevitably – some are only reproductions or partial reconstructions of the original item. They are all genuine, however, in so far as they occupy – more or less – the original site, and attempt to reproduce the actual prototype as authentically as possible.

Lastly, it behooves me to admit that this is idiosyncratic history, leaving out much of importance as well as much that is trivial. But this is a book to be browsed over – and, hopefully, enjoyed – not studied for an academic goal. Inevitably, the selection process left much to be desired, the only principle followed being the author's arbitrary choice among a library of photographs. No doubt his choice will be different from yours.

NEWFOUNDLAND

*I*nhabitants of Britain's oldest colony (1538) and Canada's youngest province (1949), Newfoundlanders have been bound to the sea in general and the inshore fishery in particular for much more than "t'ree hunnert years gone by". Even their oil is offshore oil, sucked from beneath the sea bed.

In 1493, King Henry VII of England awarded Giovanni Cabotto, a Genoese adventurer in royal service (the parochial English called him John Cabot), ten guineas – perhaps the equivalent of $50,000 in current values – for his discovery of the "new found land". But Vikings had found it – and lost it again – four hundred years before that.

Labrador, on the North American mainland, is also part of Newfoundland and may well be the first part of the continent visited by Vikings. Certainly, Basque fishermen were hunting whales off the Labrador coast in the early sixteenth century.

L'Anse aux Meadows.
A fourteenth-century Norse saga recounts how Viking adventurers from Greenland visited "Vinland" and fought with "skraelings" – perhaps Beothuk Indians – some three hundred years before that. Archaeological evidence was uncovered here in 1961, and excavations continued until 1976, exposing the sites of three wood-framed, turf-covered huts dating from about 1000 AD – the largest of them nearly eighty feet long and divided into six rooms. Associated with them were such artifacts as a bronze pin, a spindle whorl, or simple wool-spinning device, and unmistakable evidence of a blacksmith's shop.

These huts have been reconstructed on the basis of on-site archaeology and evidence gathered from chronologically parallel Viking sites in Greenland and Iceland.

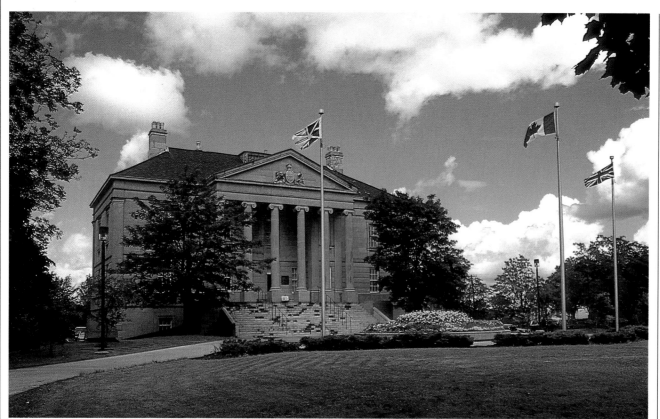

Left: Colonial Building, St. John's.
After the Great Fire of 1846 had destroyed the existing Court House, where the colonial Assembly had been meeting, it became necessary to provide it with a new home. Built in the Classical Revival style out of imported white limestone (from Cork, in Ireland), this impressive structure – its architecture in no way related to the island ethos – was "to become the scene of some of the most stormy, fatal and tragic moments in Newfoundland history."

In the late 1950s, taking advantage of federal money, the government built a new, slab-sided, Confederation Building – all glass and concrete and brick, its appearance quite unrelated to the island ethos – designed to house a vastly-expanded bureaucracy as well as the Assembly. Of course, it was soon too small as well.

Right: **Court House, St. John's.**
Yet another wooden Court House, the third of its kind, was destroyed by fire in 1892 and replaced, in 1904, with this sturdy neo-Romanesque building boasting a city clock. The cornerstone was laid by Prince George (later King George V) when he visited the colony in 1901.

Public clocks were important when only the well-to-do could afford pocket watches and no one had yet devised the wristwatch.

Facing page bottom: **Cabot Tower, St. John's.**
Built on Signal Hill, overlooking St. John's landlocked harbour, to commemorate the 400th anniversary of John Cabot's discovery of Newfoundland in 1497, the tower was used by Guglielmo Marconi to receive the first trans-Atlantic radio transmission (broadcast in Morse from Poldhu, in Cornwall, England) in 1901. His receiving aerial was a 150-metre wire lifted by a kite, and it took the best part of a month's experimentation to get those first few dots and dashes across the ocean.

Right: **Lighthouse, Cape Spear.**
Standing on the most easterly point of the North American continent, an oil-burning light first shone from the top of a stubby stone tower protruding through the roof of the lightkeeper's home in 1836. The first lighthouse, carefully restored, can be seen in the background. The present concrete tower was completed in 1955 to accommodate an electric version of the original light, and it is still maintained by a direct descendant of the man appointed lightkeeper in 1845.

Below: **Coastal Defence Battery, Cape Spear.**
This gun emplacement was constructed for one of two 10-inch naval guns installed during the Second World War to protect Canadian soil from the marauding Hun. Beneath the gun sites, underground passages linked them with a complex of magazines and equipment stores.

Although U-boats operated in the Gulf of St. Lawrence (and a surfaced Japanese submarine allegedly fired a shot or two at British Columbia's Estevan Point Lighthouse) none of our numerous coastal batteries were ever fired in anger.

Right: **Anglican Church, Fogo Island**.

Although the island, off Newfoundland's northeastern coast, has been settled since the early 1700s, well-meaning but inept civil servants in St. John's and Ottawa wanted to move all the island's inhabitants to the so-called mainland in the resettlement madness which marked the 1960s. They were thwarted by determined islanders who (temporarily) abandoned their traditional religious, social and cultural rivalries in order to frustrate a common enemy. Once there were more than twenty communities on Fogo Island; there are still ten, not prosperous, but apparently content.

Left: ***Grenfell Monument, St. Anthony.***

Sir Wilfred Grenfell (1865-1940), an English missionary doctor, built hospitals, an orphanage and nursing stations along the remote Newfoundland and Labrador coasts and sponsored the first fishing co-operatives.

The Grenfell Missions in Labrador were as famous in their day as that of Dr. Albert Schweitzer in Lambarene (French Equitorial Africa) a generation later – but few remember either any more!

Left: **Old Rolling Stock, Grand Falls.**

A narrow-gauge railway once crossed Newfoundland from St. John's to Port-aux-Basques, its slow and stately (and sometimes irregular) ways earning it affectionate recognition as "the Newfie bullet." Completion of the trans-Canada Highway and declining revenues led to its replacement with a trans-island bus service in the 1960s.

Below: **Lobster Cove Head Lighthouse.**

Older Newfoundland lighthouses were built of wood or cast iron, more modern ones of concrete. This one, constructed of iron in 1897, stands on the north side of Bonne Bay, in Gros Morne National Park along Newfoundland's French shore. There are still twenty-six cast-iron lighthouses remaining in the province out of the thirty-eight which once existed.

THE MARITIMES

*R*eason and economics demand that Nova Scotia, New Brunswick and Prince Edward Island – encompassing less than 1% of Canada between them, with a combined gross domestic product amounting to less than a sixth of Ontario's – become one. Tradition and prejudice ensure otherwise, however. An unfortunate coincidence brought the Maritime provinces into Confederation during that little span of time when technological changes in the world at large were inevitably affecting two of them very much for the worse; and Confederation has done little to alter their circumstances for the better. Thus economic prosperity has been as rare in the land of "wooden ships and iron men" as human talent has been common. Joshua Slocum, the first man to sail around the world single-handed, was a Nova Scotian; Bonar Law, British prime minister 1922-23, and newspaper magnate and political dilettante Max Aitken, who became Lord Beaverbrook and made and unmade British governments, were both New Brunswickers by birth; Prince Edward Island, on the other hand, had Lucy Maud Montgomery …

Below: **Habitation Port Royal, Nova Scotia**.
Founded by Pierre Du Gua, sieur de Monts, in 1605, on the Fundy shore of present-day Nova Scotia, this was where Samuel de Champlain organized the first North American country club, *L'Ordre de Bon Temps*, to while away the long winter evenings of his men. Until 1610, there were no women at Port Royal, the only European settlement north of Spanish Florida.

No gold, either, but members took turns at providing fresh meat through the hunting of local game and, as chief steward of the day, at leading a ceremonial procession to the table. "We passed this winter most joyously," wrote Champlain, "and fared lavishly."

Above, above left and left:
Governor's House, Port Royal.
The governor's quarters were comfortable, if not palatial; and through his leaded windows he could keep a watchful eye on some of his Acadian subjects – one of whom might well have been fabricating cedar shakes for his roof.

These buildings are all reconstructions, of course, based on descriptions and drawings by Champlain and Marc Lescarbot, and on an archaeological survey of the site.

Right: **Officers' Quarters, Fort Anne, Nova Scotia.**
After its destruction by the English in 1613, Port Royal was rebuilt fifteen yeas later, some eight kilometres distant in a more strategically advantageous location. The new settlement was captured by the English in 1710 and renamed Annopolis Royal. Through a gateway in the wall of Fort Anne (garrisoned by British troops until 1854) can be seen a restoration of the old officers' quarters.

Below: **Acadian Village, Mont Carmel, Prince Edward Island.**
Acadian communities bespattered the Atlantic coast in the first half of the seventeenth century. Since the British carefully destroyed them all in the course of the expulsions, this is yet another reconstruction.

Above: **Grand Pré National Historic Site, Nova Scotia**. Frenchmen from Port Royal moved to this rich, marshy farmland of the Minas basin in the 1680s and stayed on after France ceded Acadia to Britain in 1713. In the 1750s, in the course of yet another Anglo-French war, most Acadians – all the British could catch – were deported, and their communities obliterated.

This unconsecrated church of Saint Charles was constructed in 1922 upon the site of the original church. The statue in front of it is a depiction of Evangeline, the heroine of Henry Wadsworth Longfellow's epic poem of 1848, which did much to spur an Acadian revival among those who had avoided expulsion in 1755.

Facing page and right: **La Forteresse de Louisbourg, Cape Breton, Nova Scotia.**

King Louis XV ordered the fortress's construction on the western tip of Cape Breton Island, to guard the Gulf of St. Lawrence and the approaches to Québec, and a small town grew up around it. The British attacked twice, in 1745 and 1758, and both times town and fortress were taken. After the Conquest of Québec in 1759, the abandoned settlement soon became a deserted and forlorn monument to French industry and British seapower, crumbling into ruin through the precipitation and frost of Cape Breton winters. Preservation began in 1928, and reconstruction in the early 1960s, restoring the fortress and a part of the town to the (somewhat idealized) conditions of 1744.

Below: **Louisbourg Buildings, Cape Breton.**

About a fifth of the town has been renewed. These outlying houses loom through a mist typical of the harsh climatic cycles that quickly crumbled eighteenth-century mortar, and split and tumbled carefully crafted masonry.

Above: **Citadel Hill, Halifax, Nova Scotia.**
The British equivalent of Louisbourg was Halifax – and the key structure in its defences was the star-shaped Citadel overlooking the harbour and the entrance to Bedford Basin. The present fort (earlier works were built in 1749-50, 1776-81 and 1795-1800) was constructed between 1828 and 1856, but was noticeably disintegrating even before it was finished!

Left: **Old Town Clock, Halifax.**
Predating the present Citadel, this curious old clock, installed at the behest of George III's youngest son, Prince Edward (who was commander in chief of his father's troops in British North America at the time), stands on the slopes of Citadel Hill where it has been chiming the hours since 1803. It was fortunately situated on that side of the hill protected from the blast of the Halifax explosion of 1917 (the world's largest man-made blast before Hiroshima, in 1945), which levelled most of the city's north end and killed or injured one in five of the population.

Right: **Town Crier, Halifax.**
In the days when only a small proportion of the population could read and there were no electronic news media, the town crier was an essential part of every major community. Now his role is largely symbolic, but tradition dies hard.

Facing page: **Christ Church Cathedral, Fredericton, New Brunswick.**
Founded by loyalists, Anglican beliefs and values were at the core of this "haven for the King's friends" when Fredericton was established in 1783. The magnificent cathedral, constructed between 1846 and 1853, symbolized the political as well as the religious roots of the community.

Right: **All Souls' Chapel, Charlottetown, Prince Edward Island.**
The same faith, but a smaller, simpler, less threatened way of life, is manifest in the interior of this little chapel.

Facing page top: **Province House, Charlottetown.**
Home of the Prince Edward Island legislature, and of the Confederation Chamber, this Classical Revival building lends a certain air of elegance to Charlottetown. Named after Queen Charlotte, wife of George III, the town was chosen to be the capital when the colony's status as an entity separate from Nova Scotia was established by British fiat – at the behest of loyalists who (rightly) thought that Nova Scotia was barely loyal – in 1799.

Right: **Ardgowan House, Parkdale, Prince Edward Island.**
Exhausted by all that talking, the Fathers of Confederation refreshed themselves here, at the home of William Henry Pope, built, at least in part, from the profits of "a controversial real-estate transaction in which he and three associates made more than $10,000 at the expense of his employer."

Pope was an ardent supporter of Confederation, an attitude which drove him out of the Prince Edward Island Cabinet in 1866; but when the Island joined Confederation – out of economic necessity – in 1873, prime minister John A. Macdonald made him a judge.

Facing page bottom: **Old Wharf, St. Peters, Nova Scotia.**
On a narrow isthmus separating the Atlantic Ocean from Bras d'Or Lake at St. Peters, from 1670, boats on wooden rails were skidded less than a kilometre overland to avoid the dangerous voyage around Cape Breton proper to Glace Bay. A canal was built in 1869 providing water access from the Atlantic to the interior of Cape Breton Island, and most especially to the coalfields of Sydney and Glace Bay. The town lost its *raison d'être*, however, with the coming of bigger and more seaworthy cargo ships, and its prosperity diminished even more when a causeway at Canso linked the island to the Nova Scotian mainland in 1955. The canal now only handles pleasure boats.

Above left: **Mount Allison University, Sackville, New Brunswick.**
After a spell as a boys' school, owned and operated by the Methodist Church, Mount Allison College granted its first degrees in 1863. Not nearly as conservative as its location might suggest, in 1875 it conferred the first baccalaureate awarded to a woman in the British Empire, and in 1882 Harriet Starr Stewart received the first BA earned by a woman in Canada.

Facing page bottom: **Farmers' Bank, South Rustico, Prince Edward Island.**

The local parish priest, Father Georges-Antoine Belcourt, built this simple sandstone building between 1861 and 1864 to house North America's first client-owned bank. Behind itstands the local church, an interesting but not altogether unusual juxtaposition of God and Mammon. These farmers' banks were really savings and loan co-operatives.

Above: **Dory Shop, Shelburne, Nova Scotia.**

A flat-bottomed, amazingly seaworthy boat for two men to row and fish from, the dory was a key component of both the inshore and offshore fisheries until the advent of steam trawlers offshore and fibreglass boats inshore. Removable thwarts, or seats, allowed dories to be nested upside down on the decks of Grand Banks fishing schooners.

This shop closed as a commercial venture in 1971, after ninety years of dory building; today it is operated – nostalgically, and no doubt unprofitably – by the Shelburne Historical Society.

Left: **King's Landing, New Brunswick.**
Artifacts from all over the province, spanning a period of 150 years or more, have been assembled on the south bank of the Saint John River, above Fredericton, in this outdoor museum, which provides a concise rural history of the province. More than seventy restored buildings include a school, general store, inn, church, blacksmith's shop, water-powered sawmill, carpenter's shop, prosperous merchant's home, farms and labourers' cottages – and all the paraphernalia thereof.

Right: **Green Gables, Cavendish, Prince Edward Island.**
Great literature it is not, but *Anne of Green Gables* is surely the most widely acclaimed piece of Canadian fiction, having been translated into at least fifteen languages, including Japanese! This is the Prince Edward Island farmhouse from which the lively, red-haired Anne made the "bright passage" from childhood into adolescence which has charmed millions of readers.

Facing page bottom: **Montgomery Home, New London, Prince Edward Island.**
Anne's creator, Lucy Maud Montgomery, was born and raised here, practically next door to Green Gables. Anne is her enduring monument, but she published twenty-one other novels, an autobiography, and a vast number of poems and short stories before her death in Toronto in 1942.

Above: **Covered Wooden Bridge, Hartland, New Brunswick.**

The roofs of covered, or "kissing", bridges protected the main structure (and those using it, for whatever purpose) from the worst ravages of winter weather. In summer, of course, they simply provided cover from view and a helpfully dim and secluded environment, only tainted by people who actually wanted to cross the river!

This bridge, spanning the Saint John River, claims to be the longest in the world at 391 metres.

Right: **Steel Arch Bridge, Grand Falls, New Brunswick.**

Less romantic, and more utilitarian, than any covered wooden bridge. Once upon a time, Grand Falls was a tourist trap not unlike Niagara Falls, but in the 1920s a dam and generating station substantially reduced the spectacle that gorge and falls presented and Grand Falls now depends largely upon local agriculture – mostly potatoes, destined to become frozen french fries – for whatever prosperity it has.

Left: *"Beinn Bhreagh," Baddeck, Nova Scotia.*

Alexander Graham Bell (1847-1922) came to Canada from Scotland at the age of twenty-three, moved to the United States in 1872, and made a fortune from his many damnable inventions – especially the telephone – and through his marriage to heiress Mabel Hubbard. He bought land for a summer home at Baddeck in 1890 and spent much of his later life here at "Beinn Bhreagh" (the Gaelic for "beautiful mountain") on the shores of Bras d'Or Lake.

In the bay below, with Bell's financial backing and moral support, the Aerial Experiment Association experimented with hydrofoil boats in 1908; on shore, its Silver Dart, flown by J.A.D. McCurdy, made the first aeroplane flight in the British Empire on 23 February 1909.

Above: BLUENOSE II, *Halifax, Nova Scotia.*

Canada's most famous ship and the Maritimes' most notable symbol, the original *Bluenose* was launched at Lunenburg in 1921. She won the International Fisherman's Trophy for the fastest sailing ship of the North Atlantic fishing fleets in 1921, 1922 and 1923, and again in 1931 and 1938. Sold to a West Indies trading company in 1942, she was wrecked off Haiti in 1946.

This replica was built in the same shipyard as the original and launched in 1963. It, too, now needs replacing.

QUÉBEC

*T*hough their forefathers were virtually abandoned by their European kin from 1760 until Charles de Gaulle shouted "*Vive le Québec Libre*" from the balcony of Montréal's City Hall on 24 July 1967, *les québécois* have clung resolutely to their French heritage. Their culture was built on rock, not sand, and has not fallen yet; but, inevitably, theirs is a losing cause.

It is a measure of French Canada's communal desperation that its government now legislates language and culture, but the tides of progress, driven by science and technology and economics, are running against them. Somewhere in the indefinite future a bell is tolling for *les habitants*. In the meantime, their distinctiveness gives Canada much of *its* distinctiveness; and their loss will be our loss.

In every other way Québec prospers. With the federal government's gift of eastern Rupert's Land in 1912, the province came to occupy more than 15% of Canadian territory, making it the largest of all the provinces and three times the size of France! Its gross domestic product is five times that of the three Maritime provinces combined, and its enormous hydro-electric potential – concentrated in one-time Rupert's Land – brightens a future in which demands for energy multiply every year.

Above and facing page: **Lighthouse, Cap de Rosiers.**

At thirty-seven metres, with its stone walls more than two metres thick at the base and half that at the top, this is the tallest lighthouse in Canada. Built in 1854, its light shines far out to sea from a height of forty-four metres above sea level.

From here, almost a hundred years earlier, a French officer saw a fleet approaching and sent the news posthaste to Québec. But without a local pilot, who could navigate a fleet of clumsy, square-rigged men of war up the treacherous, shoal-infested St. Lawrence? Master-navigator James Cook, worthy successor to Jacques Cartier, could and did, taking Major General James Wolfe and 8,500 British soldiers with him.

Left: **Blanchette Homestead, Anse Blanchette.**

Settling on the Gaspé shore, close to where Cartier had raised his cross, an extended Blanchette family fished, farmed and forested, making themselves virtually self-sufficient in their daily lives, archetypes of the traditional French Canadians. Such things as ploughs and axe-heads had to be imported, but even the most sophisticated tools were simple and lasted for generations.

Modern medicine might have improved their lives in some respects, but taken by and large their lifestyles were probably as close to paradise as the climate would permit. No cars, no telephones, no radios or televisions. On the other hand, no books either!

Right: **Baie Ste. Claire, Anticosti.** The first settlement on the island abandoned in the 1920s, Baie Ste. Claire is now a ghost town, a perfect symbol of Anticosti's history. The latter's name comes from an Indian word, *natiscosti*, meaning "where the bears are hunted." Cartier discovered it, Louis Joliet was rewarded with it for his Mississippi explorations, the British annexed it to Newfoundland in 1762, and then gave it to Canada in 1774. In the end, nobody much wanted it.

A population of some 3,000 in the late 1920s has dwindled to 300, on an island 225 kilometres long and fifty wide, but wilderness is now coming into fashion for its own sake and Anticosti is making a subdued comeback as a nature park and game preserve.

Facing page bottom: **Porte St. Louis, Québec.**

When the St. Lawrence was the only gateway to Canada's interior, Québec – where cannon could command the narrowing river from the heights of Cap-Diamant – was the key. Its massive walls, now pierced by a dozen gates, or portes (of which this one, on the Grande Allée, was always the most important), stretch for some four and a half kilometres around the old city.

In the 1870s progressive thinkers sought to tear them down and several gates, including this one, were demolished to ease the flow of horse-drawn traffic! A new governor general, Lord Dufferin, forbade such barbarism and, happily, they have since been restored.

Left and below: **Champlain Monument and Lower Town, Québec.**

This statue of Samuel de Champlain, "father of New France" and governor of the infant colony from 1633 until his death two years later, looks down upon a community very different from that which he created. But the relationships he developed with the Indians – an alliance with the Hurons, incurring the enmity of the Iroquois – probably played a greater part in determining North American history than anything he did among his own people.

Left: **Château Frontenac, Québec.**
Reflected in the sunglasses of an intrigued tourist, this great hotel has welcomed kings of sovereign states, as well as princes of commerce and industry and statesmen of international renown, since 1893.

US President Franklin Roosevelt and British Prime Minister Winston Churchill both stayed here as guests of the Canadian government in 1943 and 1944, while settling Second World War grand strategy. It was an appropriate venue, for the grand strategies of Louis de Buade, Comte de Frontenac, governor of New France for twenty years between 1672 and his death in 1698, had once dictated the course of empire in North America much as Roosevelt's and Churchill's dictated the course of world events after their time.

Above: **Carleton Memorial, Québec.**
This plaque, set into the cliffs below the city, commemorates Guy Carleton, Lord Dorchester, who really ought to be French Canada's greatest hero. First appointed governor in 1766 – leaving in 1778, but returning for another three-year term in 1793 – he favoured the traditional culture and religion of *les habitants*, laying a post-conquest foundation for their survival in an age when such toleration was as uncommon as it was unexpected. Then, of course, came Lord Durham ("Radical Jack") in 1838, to report on "two nations warring in the bosom of a single state" – the French being " an old and stationary society in a new and progressive world … a people with no history and no literature."

Views of Old Québec.
The Lower Town (*above*), situated along the riverfront at the foot of the cliff, was the site of Champlain's original fort, built in 1608, and thus the oldest site of the city itself. After a chequered history, it has been the subject of a government rebuilding and restoration policy that would render the area recognisable to its eighteenth-century inhabitants and has certainly made it popular with present-day residents and tourists alike. The narrow, crowded streets of both the Lower Town and old uptown Québec are best explored either on foot or in one of the many *calèches* (*right*) that exist for this specific purpose. These quaint reminders of horse-drawn days serve only to enhance the romantic, nostalgic atmosphere of old Québec. It is ironic then that Château Frontenac (*facing page*), which so dominates the old city, celebrates a more modern, more prosaic means of transport.

*Left: **Basilica, Ste-Anne-de-Beaupré.*** Towering over the little hamlet of Ste-Anne, this enormous basilica, dating from 1926, stands on the site of three earlier shrines. The most famous pilgrimage site in North America, with more than a million visitors each year, the physical apposition of shrine and hamlet illustrates very clearly the traditional French Canadian relationship between church and state, broken so rudely in the 1950s and '60s.

*Above: **"Sugaring Off," Cookshire.*** The splendid simplicity of a boiling cauldron of sap in a grove of sugar maples contrasts with the simple splendour of an altar in St. Anne's basilica. This traditional cupola-topped wooden sugar camp, typical of hundreds found throughout rural Quebec, dates back to the 1890s, long before acid rain started to take its toll on the maple industry.

Left: **Fort Chambly, Chambly.**
A restoration of the original fort, which was erected on the west bank of the Richelieu River in 1665 (initially as Fort St. Louis), to defend the infant colony against Iroquoian -and, later, Anglo-American – raids.

Intended to block any approach along the strategic Hudson-Richelieu valleys between New York and New France, it was never strong enough to resist a major assault, and fell to the British in 1760, to the Americans in 1775, and to the British again in 1776.

Below left: **Fort Lennox, Ile aux Noix.**
Named after Charles Lennox, Duke of Richmond and Lennox and Governor in Chief of British North America (who died of rabies in 1819, after being bitten by a fox), Fort Lennox lies on an island first entrenched by the French in 1760 to block a British advance on Montréal.

After the American Revolution, the British began to fortify the island, with earthern walls and a flooded ditch, or moat, to protect the interior structures. Commanding the exit from Lake Champlain, any attack on the fort had to come by means of wooden boats – a mode of transportation especially vulnerable to red-hot cannonballs. Stoves to heat them, like the one in the foreground, were thus a key element in Fort Lennox's defences.

Facing page: **Haskell Opera House, Rock Island.**
A more peaceful atmosphere prevailed when this replica of the Boston Opera House, straddling the border, was built in 1904. Spectators sit in the United States watching the actors play their parts on a Canadian stage – the "undefended border" marked by a black line painted on the floor!

Right: **Les Forges du Saint Maurice, Trois Rivières.**

Nearby iron ore deposits made Saint Maurice the site of Canada's first heavy industry from 1738, with a blast furnace and two forges. The "most technically advanced ironworks in America" for nearly a hundred years, these forges produced stoves and agricultural and domestic implements, and, latterly, wheels for railcars, but experiments in steel making and cannon-founding were "not fruitful."

The last furnace cooled in 1883 but its memory is rekindled for visitors through this life-like bas-relief in a national park's on-site display.

Facing page: **Old Mill, Standbridge East.**

A far older Canadian "industry" than iron founding is represented by this nineteenth-century mill on the banks of the Rivière de Brochets Nord. The Cornell mill, dating from 1830, now forms part of the Missisquoi County Museum.

Left: **Place Jacques Cartier, Montréal.**

A much-changed Hochelaga commemorates the first European to cast his eyes upon it in a downtown square carefully restored to its Confederation-era splendour. By then, Montréal was the commercial and economic centre of Canada – a title subsequently usurped by Toronto.

Above: **Maisonneuve Memorial, Montréal.**

Looming between the twin towers of old Montréal's "parish church" of Notre-Dame, is this statue of the city's founder, Paul de Chomedey, sieur de Maisonneuve, who began construction of Notre-Dame de Ville-Marie de Montréal on 18 May 1642. The church, however, only dates from 1829.

Inside, a majestic altar (*right*) is lit by sunshine filtering through stained glass. The western tower houses one of North America's largest bells, the twelve-ton "Gros Bourdon."

Left: **Saint-Sulpice Seminary, Montréal.**
Granted the whole island of Montréal as their seigneury (they held it for nearly two hundred years – had they held on, what would the Order be worth today?) the first Sulpicians arrived in 1657. Their particular vocation was the training of parish priests. Their seminary, built in 1685, is Montréal's oldest building, and its clock is recognized as North America's oldest public clock.

Left and below: **Château Ramezay, Montréal.**
Built in 1705, the home of Montréal's eleventh governor, Claude de Ramezay, is now a museum re-creating the contemporary opulence of a French gentleman's home in the mid-eighteenth century. It once served as headquarters for the American army, which occupied Montréal in the winter of 1775-76, when Benjamin Franklin made great efforts to convert the French Canadians to democracy.

Right: **Stone Ruins, Ile Sainte-Thérèse.**

Still standing end-walls and chimneys suggest that this was once a typical habitant homestead on what was once a prosperous seigneury. Today, they might serve as an archetypal memorial to a way of life gone for ever.

Below: **Bishop's University, Lennoxville.**

'Artsy' from its beginnings, Bishop's was founded in 1843 by George Jehoshaphat Mountain (now there's a name for the ages!) Québec's third Anglican bishop, to "provide a liberal education for English-speaking Lower Canada, and to train Anglican clergy." Built in the "Oxbridge" tradition, this is McGreer Hall, the central structure in Canada's smallest, but far from slightest, university.

*Right: **McGill University, Montréal.*** There was much judicial dispute between his heirs over a bequest by fur trader and Scottish merchant-prince James McGill which he had directed to the financing of an English-language institute of higher learning. The matter was not settled until 1821, when McGill University was founded, to the vast frustration of its benefactor's family.

The new university specialized in medicine in its early years (acquiring a Faculty of Medicine before it established a Faculty of Arts) and it has always been noted for its medical research. But the oldest building on campus is this Arts Building, dating from 1843.

Right: **Notre-Dame de Bonsecours, Montréal.**

The first "sailor's chapel," dedicated to Notre-Dame de Bonsecours, was built in the 1660s to the order of Marguerite Bourgeoys, founder of the Congrégation de Notre-Dame. Destroyed by fire in 1745, it was rebuilt in 1772 and restored in 1888. The little observation balcony in the spire offers a panoramic view of old Montréal.

Right: **City Hall, Montréal.**

Originally built (1872-78) in a baroque Second Empire style, it was rebuilt in 1922 following the usual fire.

Below: **Fire Station, Montréal.**

Fire has always been the bane of Canadian communities – perhaps an inevitable concomitant of rough construction and cold winters. And if shipwrecked mariners traditionally worshipped in a rebuilt Notre-Dame de Bonsecours, then this renovated nineteenth-century business house, serving now as a fire station in old Montréal, might well prove a suitable shrine for flame-scourged landsmen.

Above and facing page: **Laurier Home, St. Lin-des-Laurentides.** A vain, ambitious lawyer and journalist, and a "pragmatic" politician, the much-respected Wilfrid Laurier – he has been taken as a symbol of two nations living peaceably in a single state – lived here as a child.

Vigorously opposing Confederation, Laurier entered politics in 1865 (through the radical Parti Rouge), and switched to federal Liberalism as an MP in 1874 ("more a skilful politician than a sincere defender of the Catholic minority"), becoming the seventh prime minister of Canada ("he would allow nothing to check his ambitions") from 1896 to 1911.

Appropriately enough, when Ontario's Waterloo Lutheran University decided to become a secular institution in 1973 it discovered a way to make good use of its existing initials, and is now Wilfrid Laurier University. The old trimmer would surely have appreciated the pragmatism of that.

Protestant Churches, Eastern Townships.
Predominantly French-speaking and Roman Catholic for more than four hundred years, rural Québec has had its English-speaking, Protestant enclaves – most notably in the Eastern Townships – for half that time. The United Church in Baldwin's Mills (*left*) is typical of the genre; so was the old Congregational Church (*facing page*), now a church museum, in Eaton.

English names are tolerated – for the moment – but English grammar has become blasphemous to the new Québec. In one of its bizarre attempts at language preservation, the government has decreed the abolition of that Anglo iniquity, the apostrophe: so that Baldwin's Mills is now officially Baldwin Mills.

A Brief History of Transportation in Québec.

Draft teams lined up for inspection and judgement at a country fair recall the transportation system of an earlier day, although the first such teams were probably composed of oxen rather than horses. Then came the railway, its one-time economic power and influence underlined by the now-decaying majesty of Montréal's Windsor Station; and then the automobile, although this parade of early Ford cars bears little resemblance to those that clog the streets in the rush hour today. Waterborne transport has always played a major role in Canadian economics, and the St. Lawrence Seaway, opened in 1959, enabled ore-carriers and ocean-going freighters to reach into the very heart of Canada, at the head of Lake Superior – thus diminishing Montréal's status as a major port.

Right: **Business in Montréal.**
Labelled the city's first skyscraper when it was built in 1887, the New York Life Insurance Company's new building rose all of *eight* storeys into the heavens! No longer a skyscraper, appropriately enough it now houses *La Société de Fiducie du Québec.*

Left and facing page: **Village Store, Compton.**
Now, of course, a memorial to Louis St. Laurent, twelfth prime minister of Canada (from 1948 to 1958), whose father built this store in 1866. St. Laurent, born in 1882, was a very different kind of man from Laurier: he was a corporation lawyer and law professor who had no desire to become a politician, still less a prime minister, and only did so from a sense of duty, not ambition.

Left: **Benedictine Chapel, St. Benoît-du-Lac.**
This little chapel belongs to the far grander abbey at St. Benoît, still home to more than sixty monks. The abbey was designed by Dom Paul Bellot, a French Benedictine who came to Canada in 1936 and was also responsible for the cupola on Montréal's St. Joseph's Oratory.

Facing page: **St. Joseph's Oratory, Montréal.**
A city landmark on the slopes of Mont-Royal, dedicated to the patron saint of Canada. Construction of the basilica (in the Beaux-Arts style) was begun during the First World War, largely at the instigation of Brother André, beatified in 1982, whose statue stands beside the finished shrine. Another monument to a world that has passed.

Left: ***Christ Church Cathedral, Montréal.***
Dwarfed by the massive towers of modern business, a quiet island in an ocean of traffic, the Anglican cathedral of Montréal, built between 1849 and 1857, endures as a seemingly irrelevant sepulchre of the English and Anglican tradition in Québec. Like many another church or chapel in a largely post-Christian age, it is now noted more for its Gothic styling and stained glass than for its religious significance.

Above: **Le Forum de Montréal.**
The contemporary cathedral of Québec. Built in 1924, the home ice of "les glorieux," packed – as on nearly every "Hockey Night in Canada" – with 16,000 fervent fans and with television cameras carrying an instantaneous electronic image to all those unfortunates left out in the cold. A house of prayer to the gods of sport? How ironic, then, that many of the saints should be English-speaking – and some of them Americans!

OTTAWA
THE NATION'S CAPITAL

*O*nce a construction site, then a lumber town, Ottawa was chosen as the capital of Canada (East and West) by a compromise edict of Queen Victoria ten years before Confederation. Ottawa itself is still part of Ontario, but the so-called National Capital Region of which it is the core extends across the Ottawa River into the province of Québec; and much of the administrative pith which defines any capital is now to be found upon the Québec bank of the Ottawa, in the curious community of Hull.

Somewhere, a bureaucratic statistician is puzzling over how to assign exactly 24.7% (or whatever the current percentage of French Canadians in the population is, all those of other racial origin being lumped together) of the geological, geographical, biological, chemical, cultural and economic aspects of Ottawa/ Hull to the heirs of Cartier and Champlain. Everything about Ottawa is true, except the facts and figures.

Left and far left: **Parliament Buildings, Ottawa.**
Construction of a home for the legislature of the united province of Canada, on a bluff overlooking the Ottawa River in a somewhat jaunty Gothic Revival style, began in 1859, and was conveniently completed in 1867, just in time to house the parliament of the new Dominion.

In 1916 fire destroyed the Centre Block, housing the Senate and Commons chambers. It was rebuilt between 1916 and 1927, along rather more stern, less romantic lines, with a taller (44.5 metres) central tower, first called the Victory Tower (the original had been the Victoria Tower but, after all, we had played a notable part in winning the First World War since then), and finally named the Peace Tower in 1933.

Above: **Peace Tower, Parliament Buildings.**
Canada's most famous clock, each of its four faces measuring nearly five metres across. Behind it lie the fifty-two bells of the Dominion Carillon, the largest weighing 544, the smallest 4.5, kilograms. Over it floats a Canadian flag, adopted – after much controversy – in 1965. Beneath it lies a Memorial Chamber, where are recorded (in a copperplate script) the names of Canada's war dead, one page of the book being turned each day.

Above and facing page: **Rideau Canal, Ottawa.**

The only obvious reason for Ottawa's existence in the first place, the Rideau Canal was constructed between 1826 and 1832 to provide an alternative route between Montréal and Kingston for military resources needed on the lower Great Lakes in the event of war between Great Britain and the United States. The community which grew up around the northern terminus of the Canal was called Bytown, after Colonel John By, the Royal Engineer officer who planned and directed its construction.

No longer useful militarily or commercially, the Canal is now used by pleasure boaters in summer and, in Ottawa at least, by recreational skaters in winter. Clearing the first seven kilometres of snow makes it the "world's longest skating rink" in the popular mind.

*Left: **Canal Locks, Ottawa.***
Hemmed in between Parliament Hill and an appropriately neo-Gothic Château Laurier hotel, this flight of locks lifts (or lowers) boats some twenty-five metres between the Ottawa River and the first (or last) stretch of canal. A total of forty-seven locks raise water levels eighty-three metres to the height of land at Newboro, and then lower them fifty-four metres to the Cataraqui River at Kingston

*Facing page top: **Conference Centre, Ottawa.***
Unwanted railway station into unsuccessful speech factory! A masterpiece of architectural and psychological recycling turned the old Union Station into a National Conference Centre when railways were eliminated from the downtown core of Ottawa in the late 1950s.

*Facing page bottom: **Moorside Ruins, Kingsmere, Province of Québec.***
These artificial ruins were erected by prime minister Mackenzie King on his Gatineau estate in the 1930s. Here King communed with nature – and sometimes with the spirit of his dead mother! – while he successfully conducted much of the nation's business.

ONTARIO

Canada's most populous and richest province, containing its greatest city, Toronto, and the nation's capital, Ottawa. The province's name comes from an Iroquoian word meaning "beautiful water." Although there were isolated French communities – mostly along the shores of the lower Great Lakes – from the late 1600s, large-scale settlement did not begin until the end of the eighteenth century and the arrival of the United Empire Loyalists.

Settled by farmers, Ontario is now the most urbanized and industrialized province of Canada, second only to Québec in size, with a gross domestic product valued at more than two-thirds of all other provinces combined.

The province divides naturally into two parts, southern and northern, prosperity and poverty, sophistication and simplicity. Too often, Canadians – even Ontarians! – forget that Ontario stretches north to Hudson's Bay. Perhaps Henry Hudson, cast adrift in the Bay by his fearful, mutinous crew in 1611, was the first European to see what is now northern Ontario?

In that same year, 1611, nineteen-year-old Etienne Brûlé left Montréal to begin the travels which took him as far as Lake Superior by 1622 and led him over much of what is now southern Ontario. Would the first white man to have seen that vast freshwater sea and Niagara Falls have been overly impressed by the CN tower or the Skydome? Probably not. Astonished, perhaps, but not overly impressed.

Facing page top: **Sainte-Marie Among the Hurons, Midland.** Founded by French Jesuits in 1639 as a base for itinerant missionaries and a refuge for Christianized Indians. They planted gardens and fields, harvested crops previously unknown to the Indians, and imported livestock – chickens, pigs and goats, perhaps cattle – from Montréal; and more missions were established nearby.

Ten years later, one-fifth of the meagre European population of New France was to be found in the vicinity, together with several thousand Indians. Besides a church, there were farm buildings, carpenters' and blacksmiths' shops, a hospital (with an apothecary's store attached), and a cobbler's and a tailor's shop.

Facing page bottom: **Huron Longhouse, Sainte-Marie.** The Hurons, like the tribes of the Iroquois Confederacy to which they were linguistically related, were more socially sophisticated than most other tribes, and lived in longhouses framed with saplings and covered with bark or rushes. As many as twenty families might share a longhouse, each with its own space and own fire. This reconstructed one resembles very closely the one originally provided (on the same site) for Indians who became a semi-permanent part of the Sainte-Marie community.

Left: **Palisades, Sainte-Marie.** Building his fur-trade alliances, Samuel de Champlain unwittingly committed the French to the Huron cause in a long-standing rivalry between them and the Iroquois. In 1648, when the Iroquois embarked on a series of campaigns designed to concentrate European trade in their hands, they raided north to Sainte-Marie, taking and burning a number of nearby subordinate missions, making prisoners of five French missionaries and ritually torturing them to death – an occasion which, three hundred years later, gave E.J. Pratt the subject matter for his epic poem, *Bréboeuf.*

These palisades would have been a weak defence, but Sainte-Marie itself was never attacked. There were soon no Hurons there for the Jesuits to minister to, however, and the mission was withdrawn the following year.

Left: **Brock Monument, Queenston Heights.**

Québec was divided into Upper and Lower Canada in 1791 but, unlike old Québec, the new province had no self identity until the War of 1812. That conflict saw a number of American attempts to occupy Canada repulsed; and, as a by-product, it gave Upper Canadians the sense of community which comes from having done great things together. Or at least from the belief that they have done great things together.

The most significant defeat inflicted on the Americans came early in the war, at Queenston Heights, near Niagara, on 13 October 1812, when Major General Sir Isaac Brock, civil administrator of Upper Canada and commander in chief of British forces, was killed at the head of his troops. His remains were interred under a stone column erected on the battlefield in 1824, though this was blown up in 1840 by a disgruntled American sympathizer. The present monument, as likely a marker as any to the creation of Ontario, was constructed between 1853 and 1856.

Facing page: **Fort George, Niagara-on-the-Lake.**

Before the American Revolution, the British (as the French had done before them) controlled the Niagara River from a fort on the eastern bank. American independence compelled its evacuation, however, and Fort George was built on the Canadian shore between 1796 and 1799.

During the War of 1812, Fort George fell to the Americans in May 1813, only to be retaken by the British in December. In those desperate fights, the fort was so badly damaged that the British then abandoned it, concentrating their defences at nearby Fort Mississauga. It was reconstructed during the 1940s by the Niagara Parks Commission.

Right: **Fort York, Toronto.**
Toronto, at the Lake Ontario end of a portage route to Lake Huron, was the site of a fortified French fur trading post, Fort Rouillé, which stood on the present Exhibition Grounds, as early as 1750. In 1793 the lieutenant governor of Upper Canada, John Graves Simcoe, moved his capital from the vulnerable border town of Niagara and established it on the site of Fort Rouillé, calling it York and building a log fort there.

In 1811, Isaac Brock strengthened the fort but that did not save it from the Americans in April 1813, when the explosion of the magazine devastated the site. After the Americans left, the British rebuilt it, however, and in 1814 the restored defences were strong enough to persuade an American naval force to stay out of range. This reconstruction, dating from the early 1930s, is now garrisoned by students masquerading as soldiers of the time.

Right and facing page top:
Blockhouse, Merrickville.
Although the Merrickville locks were far from the American border, in Lake Ontario, the builders of the Rideau Canal still felt it necessary to provide protection for key points and constructed blockhouses at Kingston Mills, Jones' Falls, Merrickville and on the outskirts of Bytown, as it then was.

This one, constructed in 1830 with stone walls over a metre thick, was intended to house up to fifty soldiers (as well as the lockmaster and his family in the wooden second storey) and was manned in times of crisis until the 1860s. It now serves as a museum of Upper Canadiana spanning the second half of the nineteenth century.

Right: **Fort Henry, Kingston.**
Built in 1836 to protect the southern end of the new Rideau Canal. According to the original plan, there were to have been five more similar forts, three on each side of the harbour, which would have made Kingston the most powerful fortress in the western hemisphere. But the other five were never built.

As the strategic hinge of Upper Canada, and then Ontario, in the event of an American attack, Fort Henry was garrisoned by British troops until 1870 and then by Canadians until 1890.

Right: **Mackenzie House, Toronto.** In 1837-8 came the two Canadian Rebellions – attempts in both Upper and Lower Canada to upset the conservative oligarchies which dominated political life. Both unsuccessful, they nevertheless gave rise to Lord Durham's famous Report, which argued that, while the one was radical and democratic, the other was fundamentally conservative and nationalistic.

In Upper Canada the spokesman of discontent was a fiery Scottish radical, William Lyon Mackenzie (*facing page top*), a rambunctious journalist and publisher of his own newspaper who was also Toronto's first mayor and an elected member of the Assembly. When his revolt failed dismally, Mackenzie fled to the United States, but was pardoned and returned to Toronto in 1849. He died here, three years later, presumably never dreaming that his grandson, William Lyon Mackenzie King, born twelve years after his death, would be prime minister of Canada for twenty-one years.

Above: **Highland Games, Maxville.**
Kilted drummers carry on the Scottish tradition – without much Gaelic, nowadays – playing their part in an annual festival which draws people claiming Highland descent from all over North America. Once there were more MacDonalds in Glengarry than in all Scotland – more than 3,000 of them in the 1852 census, not to mention the MacKinnons, MacRaes, MacGregors, MacGillivrays, and MacLarens! The "Max" in Maxville is probably a corruption of the Macs in all those Scottish names.

Above right: **Mill, Martintown.**
Wherever there was a head of water to drive a waterwheel in Upper Canada, there was built a mill – either a sawmill or a flour mill, sometimes both.

This solid structure stands on the banks of the Raisin River in country settled by a few French Canadians after 1760 and many Scottish highlanders between 1784 and 1804, and named by the latter Glengarry, after Glen Gary in far-off Inverness.

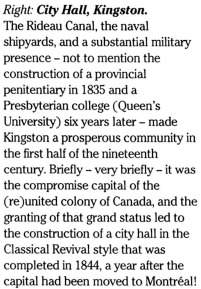

Right: **City Hall, Kingston.**
The Rideau Canal, the naval shipyards, and a substantial military presence – not to mention the construction of a provincial penitentiary in 1835 and a Presbyterian college (Queen's University) six years later – made Kingston a prosperous community in the first half of the nineteenth century. Briefly – very briefly – it was the compromise capital of the (re)united colony of Canada, and the granting of that grand status led to the construction of a city hall in the Classical Revival style that was completed in 1844, a year after the capital had been moved to Montréal!

Above: **Upper Canada Village, Morrisburg.**
The creation of the St. Lawrence Seaway in the 1950s called for the flooding of much of the old river front, including eight villages which had been among the first areas to be settled in Ontario. Moving some of the older buildings here, and adding other representative structures, the provincial government established Upper Canada Village as a replica of a mid-nineteenth-century community.

Above left: **Martello Tower, Kingston.**

Martello towers were intended to be used as protection against shipborne cannon fire and to repulse landing parties. Sixteen were built in Canada, six in the Maritimes (Halifax and Saint John), four in Québec, and six in Kingston. To handle Canadian weather better , some towers were built with removable wooden roofs.

A poor substitute for one of the proposed six Fort Henrys, this one,

eleven metres high with walls two metres thick at its base, was hurriedly constructed in 1847 at a time of renewed tension with the United States.

Far left: **Bellevue House, Kingston.**
Briefly the home of John A. Macdonald, who would in due course become the Dominion of Canada's first prime minister, this villa in an Italianate style (not generally a mainstay of Ontario architecture) was constructed in the late 1830s.

Macdonald, Kingston lawyer and member for the town in the Provincial Assembly, rented it in 1848 for his invalid wife and remarked, in a letter to his sister-in-law, on "the quiet and

seclusion of the house, which is completely surrounded with trees and has a fresh breeze ever blowing on it from Lake Ontario." No doubt it was also a good spot to take a dram of Scotch from time to time.

Left: **St. James's Cathedral, Toronto.**

The driving force behind this imposing edifice, built between 1849 and 1853, was the son of a Scottish quarryman and a bitter opponent of that other Scottish immigrant, William Lyon Mackenzie. John Strachan, first bishop of Toronto, played a notable part in the political evolution of Upper Canada after 1812, dourly defending the privileges of church and state and promoting patriarchal, "anti-American," political values.

The inexorable march of Reform overtook him, however. Perhaps the construction of St. James's and the establishment of Trinity College (now a pillar of the University of Toronto) consoled him in his old age.

Right: **St. Andrew-by-the-Lake Church, Toronto Island.**

Actually, it's fourteen islands, none of them actually called Toronto! But until 1858 Toronto Island wasn't even an island! That spring a great storm cut the sand spit joining a peninsula to the Toronto shore, making islanders of those who lived on it, psychologically as well as physically.

This charming little church, a marvellous contrast to the cathedral and, by reason of its situation, far more a haven of peace, once served some 2,000 residents; now, no more than 700. Small consolation to the remaining inhabitants that one of the fourteen islands now has its own airport.

Left: **Canadian Pacific Railway, Northern Ontario.**

The tangled country of the Laurentian Shield where it meets Lake Superior – swamp and muskeg, between rock ridges – formed as great an obstacle to the building of a trans-continental railway as did the far-mightier mountains to the west. When the North-West Field Force was ordered out in the early spring of 1885, the track was still incomplete along the north shore and troops had to march across several gaps. It was not finished until the following summer – only months before the last spike was driven, at Craigellachie, high in the Rockies, on 7 November 1885.

Left: **Old City Hall, Toronto.**
Completed in 1899, the working symbol of a city then still "remarkably homogenous, strong on church life, Sunday observance and morality." Square, turreted, neo-Gothic, it surely reflects the society which spawned it just as accurately as the concrete and glass curves of the nearby new City Hall reflect contemporary Toronto.

Above: **Township Hall, Waterloo.**
American Mennonites were the first settlers in the Waterloo area, arriving in the 1820s. How appropriate, then, is the simple "clapboard Gothic" of their rural township hall; and what a contrast with Toronto's city halls, old and new.

Above: **Town Hall, Kenora.**
Straightforward Manitobans called the place Rat Portage before an 1882 boundary dispute was resolved in Ontario's favour. More urbane easterners changed the name to Kenora, a euphonious combination of Ke-ewatin, No-rman, and Ra-t Portage, all three tiny hamlets clustered where the Winnipeg River leaves the Lake of the Woods. The railway brought it a new kind of prosperity and a handsome town hall (not quite as big as Toronto's) complete with clock.

Above: ***Refinery Stacks, Sudbury.*** Sudbury provides us with the largest single source of nickel in the world and Canada's largest source of copper. Digging out the ore, as people have been doing since 1888, six years after the builders of the Canadian Pacific Railway stumbled upon it, is no great problem, but refining it is: for many kilometres downwind of these stacks a once beautiful landscape has become as barren as the moon.

Facing page and right: **The Post Office, Renfrew, and Post Office Boxes, Bainsville.**

Now it's Canada Post, but once the Royal Mail linked the length and breadth of Canada. In those days post office boxes were made from wood, dextrously, if not lovingly, made by hand, and letters were sorted by a human being. Delivery was often quicker and junk mail was no problem, either. Mr. Eaton's catalogue had other uses, just as important to many of his customers as advertising his merchandise.

Post office and church were the centres of every community; in those happier times the Renfrew Millionaires were a power in the land and the Montréeal Canadiens or the Toronto Maple Leafs had not been invented.

Below: **Recycled Fire Hall, Unionville.**

Are there less fires than there used to be in Canada, in the last decade of the twentieth century? Or, because reports of fire travel faster and fire engines travel quicker, is it just that fire halls have become more centralized? A one-time fire station has found a new life as a sports centre. In an age when recycling is becoming *the* buzz-word, Unionville stole a march on Yuppiedom.

Right: **The Royal Conservatory of Music, Toronto.**

Founded in 1886, this opened the following year with fifty teachers and two hundred pupils on its books. Its majestic Victorian facade befits an institution which has directed – and usually dominated – the progress of music in Canada for more than a century.

Left: **Royal Alexandra Theatre, Toronto.**

Built in 1907 (at a cost of $750,000) and named in honour of Edward VII's deaf Queen, the "Royal Alex" was then, and is now – paradoxically perhaps – noted for its excellent acoustics. Yet in more modern theatres (such as Roy Thomson Hall, 1982), built with the expertise of specialized acoustical engineers readily to hand, they rarely seem to get the sound quite right.

Above: **The Flatiron Building, Toronto.**

By the 1880s land was already expensive in Toronto and no one was willing to waste it. Not even when it came in very narrow lots where two streets came together at an acute angle. Only a hundred years earlier, however, a strategic location like this would have been the site of a half-sunken fort instead of a ridiculously narrow, multi-storey business centre.

Left: *Royal Ontario Museum, Toronto.*

A hundred years ago, the southwest corner of Bloor Street and Queen's Park was a cow pasture. An ever-growing institution, physically as well as intellectually, the Royal Ontario Museum opened its doors in 1914 and now more than one and a quarter million visitors a year pass through its doors, below this *bas relief*.

Beginning as an amalgamation of five lesser museums, it has become Canada's largest museum and its best, and one of the largest in North America. Ten years ago, it held more than six million artifacts running the gamut from an Egyptian mummy, circa 1200 BC, to a contemporary Afghan lute, and from a suit of seventeenth-century English pikeman's armour to an allegorical mosaic from a fourth-century Roman Villa. Some of the exhibits are even Canadian.

Facing page: **Maid of the Mist, Niagara Falls.**

This sturdy little boat and its predecessors have carried many thousands of tourists to the spray-blurred foot of the Horseshoe Falls. Most of them found their curiosity blended inextricably with a carefully-suppressed fear that the boat would capsize; but it never has.

The photograph was taken from the grounds of Queen Victoria Park, created in 1887 "to save the area from hucksters and speculators." Fulfilling its function admirably, the park has proved to be several thousand hectares too small, however.

Left: *Retired Locomotive, Chapleau.*

Chapleau, three hundred kilometres northwest of Sudbury, in the rocky heart of the Laurentian Shield, was nothing but a decrepit Hudson's Bay Post before it was selected as a divisional point on the first trans-continental railway. Since locomotives are not recyclable, except as scrap iron, who better, then, than the citizens of Chapleau to give an old steam engine a good home?

*Left: **Seaway Lock, Iroquois.***
The first in a series of massive locks downstream from Kingston. The St. Lawrence between Montréal and Kingston was once a furious challenge to *voyageur* skills in running rapids. In the early nineteenth century, however, portages gave way to a number of small canals and locks, but it was only the construction of the St. Lawrence Seaway in the 1950s that brought uninterrupted navigation to the river for ocean-going freighters.

Above left: **HMCS Haida, Toronto.**
Moored permanently at Ontario Place, this Second World War destroyer educates Canadian children about a part of their heritage that their schools can often lose sight of in their haste to explore aboriginal cultures.

Haida was launched in 1943, spending her war years patrolling the English Channel and Bay of Biscay, playing a part in the invasion of northwest Europe and several bitterly fought sea battles. Decommissioned in 1963, she was bought from the federal government with money raised by private subscription and taken over by the provincial authorities in 1970.

Above: **Leacock Grave, Jackson Point.**
The author of *Sunshine Sketches of a Little Town, Arcadian Adventures with the Idle Rich,* and *Moonbeams from the Larger Lunacy*, as well as many lesser works, died in Toronto in 1944, but they buried Canada's greatest satirist here. Stephen Leacock opposed liberalism, materialism and the worship of technology – and he was something of a racist, too. Perhaps it was as well that he died when he did.

THE WESTERN INTERIOR

The provinces of Manitoba, Saskatchewan and Alberta form one geographic and economic unit, 20% of Canada by area and roughly equating to William Francis Butler's Great Lone Land of 1872. Long before that, however, they were all three just a part of that vast fur empire, named after King Charles II's cousin, Prince Rupert, which the Merry Monarch had given to the Hudson's Bay Company.

Across the southern plains, buffalo roamed in their millions. In the north, the land was rich in beaver, bear and marten, fox and mink.

The men who came to the fur trade, mostly from Scotland and French Canada, took Indian women to their beds and bred a mixed race who called themselves Métis, a people who evolved their own distinctive micro-culture, in many ways a life-style of fishing, hunting and farming which recalled the earliest days of European colonization.

After the British government, without consulting the inhabitants, gave Rupert's Land to Canada in 1869 – just one of the many complex bribes which brought about Confederation! – it took armed force to bring Manitoba to heel in 1870. Signing up in 1905, Saskatchewan and Alberta were, for more than half a century, (until Newfoundland took the Great Leap Forward – or was it Backward?) the youngest provinces.

When that happened, the buffalo herds were already gone, decimated by the breech-loading rifle and finally eliminated by the coming of the railway. With them went the Métis way of life. Wheat and cattle took the place of fur as the economic base of society, and more recently the destinies of two of these provinces have become tied to minerals as well: by right of oil, Alberta is the richest, Manitoba, which has no mineral resources to speak of, the poorest.

Right: **Fort Carlton, Saskatchewan.** Rivers were the highways of the fur trade and the Saskatchewan River, draining into Lake Winnipeg and then, via the Nelson River, into Hudson's Bay, was one of the greatest. "Fort" was a word rather carelessly bandied about by the fur traders, who, one suspects, fancied its impressive connotations. Carlton, on the south branch of the North Saskatchewan, was established in 1810 and it "remained a particularly important fur trade depot in western Canada" until 1882.

Left and right: **Fort Prince of Wales, Churchill, Manitoba.**

The Churchill River (named after Winston Churchill's ancestor, John Churchill, Duke of Marlborough) was a major gateway to the fur-bearing areas of Rupert's Land. The Hudson's Bay Company built a wooden fort on the northern point, close to the river mouth, in 1717, and turned it into a stone one by 1739, its sunken walls eventually guarded by forty-two cannon. Across the bay, they built a redoubt on Cape Merry, shown in the foreground (*right*).

The French had no trouble capturing it that same year, however. They spiked the cannon and blew up the buildings, and when they left (the British retaining their rights here by the Treaty of Paris, 1783) the site was left to polar bears and hawks. In the 1930s, a process of restoration and partial reconstruction was undertaken.

Right and below: **Trading Store, reconstructed Fort Carlton, Saskatchewan.**

While being evacuated during the Northwest Rebellion of 1885, Fort Carlton was accidentally set afire and burned to the ground. This is the usual tidy reconstruction, with the interior restored to indicate quite clearly what kind of a store it was. Other furs were welcome – and individually more profitable – but beaver pelts were the *raison d'être* of the fur trade, the thick underfur being used to make hats which were the height of European fashion for more than two hundred years.

Right and below: **Rocky Mountain House, Alberta.**

Further upstream, two Rocky Mountain Houses were established as early as 1799 in a fruitless attempt by both the Hudson's Bay Company and the rival Northwest Company – which had pushed west from Montréal via the Great Lakes – to reach the furs on the other side of the continental divide. Their plans never worked because the Blackfoot Confederacy, which dominated the eastern slopes, resolutely frustrated all efforts to trade with the Kootenays on the Pacific slopes. Indians were economic warriors, too.

After the Bay had absorbed its rival in 1821, John Jacob Astor's American Fur Company, expanding up the Missouri River, broke the Hudson's Bay Company's monopoly. These chimneys are all that remain of the last of a series of posts which was finally abandoned in 1875 in favour of Calgary. The interior is restored, *circa* 1825.

Right: **Upper Fort Garry, Winnipeg.**
Carrying the fur trade in another
direction, the original Fort Garry was
built at the forks of the Red and
Assiniboine rivers in 1822 – near the
site of long-lost Fort Rouge, built by
French Canadian explorer Pierre
Gaultier de Varennes, sieur de la
Vérendrye, in 1738. In 1812, Lord
Selkirk established his Red River
Colony of Scottish emigrants nearby,
initiating the distinctive Métis lifestyle
which blended hunting with farming.

The earliest fragments of this
version of Fort Garry – the fort seized
by Métis leader Louis Rield during the
so-called Red River Rebellion of 1870
– date from 1836.

Above: **Lower Fort Garry, Manitoba.**

Flooding at the Forks led the Hudson's Bay Company to establish Lower Fort Garry, thirty kilometres downstream, as the administrative headquarters for Rupert's Land in the early 1830s. But the Forks was the natural focus for the region and the Bay Company soon returned there, subsequently leasing this site to the British Army in the 1840s and to the Northwest Mounted Police (1873-4).

Right: **Trading Post, Lower Fort Garry.**

After a spell as a country club in the 1930s, the Fort was given by the Hudson's Bay Company to the federal government and ended up in the hands of Parks Canada, who set up this store as it must have been in the fort's heyday.

Right and below: **St. Boniface Museum, Manitoba.**

The oldest building in metropolitan Winnipeg is now a museum. It lies on the east bank of the Red River, right across from the Forks, in the French Canadian suburb of St. Boniface. The community was founded in 1818, after Lord Selkirk had donated land for a mission to bring the benefits of Roman Catholicism to his Highland Scots colonists and the Indians and Métis who were already putting down roots around Fort Garry.

Built of oak logs, the museum was originally a convent for the Grey Nuns, who arrived from Montréal in 1844.

Facing page: **St. Boniface College, University of Manitoba.**

Early Winnipeg architecture took the form of "Red River frame" in vertical and horizontal logs, like the old Grey Nuns' convent, but as the city grew so did its cultural aspirations. Originally *Le petit Seminaire* for aspirants to the priesthood, an earlier version of St. Boniface College was burned down in 1922 by one of those ubiquitous Canadian fires. Its replacement was built in the fashionable Classical Revival style.

The college joined Manitoba and St. John's colleges to establish the University of Manitoba in 1877, four years before the transcontinental railway reached the city.

Above and right: **Batoche, Saskatchewan.**

Driven from Red River by the onset of so-called "civilization" in 1870, numbers of diehard Métis moved northwest to settle in the valley of the North Saskatchewan. "The Métis laid their farms out in long river lot fashion, cultivating a small portion of them, but living principally by freighting, trading and raising cattle. They were a sociable people holding parties and dances in their homes … to make the long winters pass more quickly."

But civilization was not so easily denied. In 1885 came the Northwest Rebellion and, under the same Louis Riel who had led the resistance at Red River, they made a last stand at Batoche.

Illustrated here are the ruins of Garnot's inn (*right*), and the Caron farmhouse (*above*) built in the early 1890s to replace one destroyed by Canadian soldiers in the campaign.

Right: **Riel Grave, St. Boniface.**
Convicted of treason, Louis Riel was executed at Regina on 16 November 1886, but his body was taken back to his birthplace, St. Boniface, for burial. Deserved or not – and there is certainly room for argument, by the standards of that time – Riel's execution was unnecessary and only strengthened nationalist feeling in Québec. It brought about Honoré Mercier's accession to power in 1886 and moved the weight of the French Canadian vote from Tory/ Conservative to Grit/Liberal – an alignment which continued unbroken for nearly nine decades.

Above: **Portage and Main, Winnipeg.**
In 1862 a prescient Henry McKenney built his general store where the trail paralleling the Red River crossed one coming down the Assiniboine – now the most famous street corner in Canada. It is also popularly believed to be the coldest. That wise old bird, Stephen Leacock, quite rightly observed that, "With the thermometer at 30° below zero and the wind behind him, a man walking down Main Street in Winnipeg knows which side of him is which."

*Above: **Rail Yards, Winnipeg.***
The "end of steel" reached Winnipeg in 1881, but it was its extension beyond that which launched the town into an era of growth and prosperity probably still unequalled in Canadian urban development. By 1911, a community which had only had a population of 3,700 in 1874 had become the third largest city in Canada, ranking fourth in manufacturing.

*Facing page bottom: **Royal Northwest Mounted Police Post, Calgary.***
The original post was established in 1875 by Inspector E.A. Brisebois, who modestly named it Fort Brisebois; he was very shortly overruled by Colonel James Mcleod who preferred the name of his ancestral home in Scotland. Fort Calgary's life was comparatively short, however, for the arrival of the railway in 1883 and the

Left: **Post Office, Battleford, Saskatchewan.**

Battleford was the capital of the old Northwest Territories in 1876, when they encompassed all the present Territories and what are now the three prairie provinces as well. A small prairie village was suddenly the capital of more than half of present-day Canada! And then, no doubt, the mail began to pour in.

The date on the clock tower reads 1911 but Battleford was stripped of its new-found status in 1882. The Canada Pacific Railway transcontinental line, once projected to come through the town, went through south Saskatchewan instead; and when a railway did come north, in 1905, it slipped past Battleford, an event which led to the creation of neighbouring North Battleford. Was this dignified post office a federal consolation prize?

subsequent expansion of Calgary quickly made it superfluous.

This building, which housed the commanding officer's quarters, was built in 1906, and moved twice, before coming to rest close to the junction of the Elbow River with the Bow, somewhere near the spot where old Fort Calgary is now "securely buried under city concrete."

Right: **Cochrane Ranch, Cochrane, Alberta.**

With the buffalo gone, the prairies were soon leased out to livestock companies. In Canada, from the beginning, ranching was big business. This particular big business, north of Calgary, was founded in 1881 with nearly seven thousand head of cattle driven up from Montana, and eventually covered 190,000 acres – mostly leased from the federal government at one cent an acre, after Senator Matthew Cochrane had lobbied Sir John Macdonald into it.

If the owners were businessmen, their employees were genuine cowboys. Not exactly in the John Wayne mould, but near enough. Even that has changed now, in an era of ATVs and cellular phones, although this statue of a cowboy, on the "Men of Vision" viewpoint at the Cochrane Ranch, encourages visitors to recall a romantic past.

Right: **Ukrainian Church, near Edmonton.**
Tough, hardworking Ukrainian immigrants poured into Canada between 1891 and 1914, drawn to the prairies by their similarity in climate and terrain to their own familiar steppes. They homesteaded (generally in block settlements) and farmed; and mostly they grew the new wheat, marquis, which matured earlier and made the prairies the breadbasket of the world.

Facing page bottom: **Steam Engine, near Edmonton.**
Cattle followed close on the buffalo but wheat was never far behind, first Red Fife and harvesters, cereals had to be threshed by machines powered by steam engines, such as this one on display at the Ukrainian Cultural Heritage Village, near Edmonton.

Right and below: **Grain and Train, Alberta.**

Grain elevators have always been the far-off, long-visible signs of prairie prosperity. From them, great lumbering freight trains haul it away to more elevators in Thunder Bay (Fort William/Port Aurthur to an older generation) or across the Rockies to Vancouver – some of it even across the tundra to Churchill, on the frozen shores of Hudson's Bay.

Facing page: **Train and Grain, Manitoba.**

Churchill is some 1,600 kilometres closer to Europe by sea than is Montréal. In 1931 the federal government completed a railway from Winnipeg to Churchill, and then built harbour facilities which included elevators looking more like some ultra-modern cathedral than what they really are. The capacity of the port is limited by the short shipping season – three months at the most – and shallow water.

Above: **Harvest Festival, Osler, Saskatchewan.**
Saskatchewanis enthusiastically re-enact a 1930s harvest using the machinery their grandparents may have used.

Left and facing page: **Banff National Park, Alberta.**
Canada's first, and probably best-known, national park was established here in 1886, the justification being that it "presented features of the greatest natural beauty." And, indeed, it did. Witness Lake Louise, named after Princess Louise Caroline Alberta, fourth daughter of Queen Victoria and wife of Canada's governor-general at the time, the Marquis of Lorne.

Originally Lake Louise was called Emerald Lake, for more obvious reasons.

Left: **Banff Springs Hotel, Banff.**
Railway workers driving the transcontinental line towards the Pacific stumbled on the hot springs here in 1883, and a great many Canadians (and Americans and Europeans and, of recent years, Japanese) have stumbled over them since. The Canadian Pacific Railway erected a four-storey timber structure containing 250 rooms ($3.50 a day, including meals, but wine was extra) and opened it in 1888. Despite the shockingly high prices, it was an instant success. The present hotel, of concrete-clad steel with stone facing, dates from 1928, and in 1988 the least expensive room cost $95 without either meals or wine.

Facing page bottom: **Abandoned Harvester near Fielding, Saskatchewan.**
For the wheat farmer on the prairies, the "dirty thirties" of the Great Depression were a combination of economic recession and drought, striking him a double blow. The Second World War brought boom times back, but since then growing grain has been an up-and-down business. Perhaps it was depressed grain prices which led some farmer to abandon this old machine where he last had occasion to use it; and then again, perhaps it was sheer laziness.

Left: **Oil Well, Calgary, Alberta.**
Where the buffalo once roamed freely and cattle still graze, horsehead pumps nod and bow rhythmically. The first commercial exploitation of petroleum in Canada developed in southwest Ontario in the late 1850s and the first western production came from Alberta's Turner Valley in 1910, but by 1946 Canadian wells were still only furnishing 10% of domestic consumption. Then, on 13 February 1947, Imperial Oil struck it rich at Leduc. Today, Canada could be self-sufficient in oil if only most of it was not owned (and exported to you-know-where) by American companies.

BRITISH COLUMBIA
AND THE YUKON

If Labrador was, as Jacques Cartier suggested, "the land God gave to Cain" then coastal British Columbia might well have been the fields (vineyards?) he left with Abel! Basking in a maritime climate, 70% of British Columbia's population is concentrated in the beautiful and fertile Lower Mainland and on the southeast corner of Vancouver Island. The interior of the province blends imperceptibly into the north, however, and that leads to the Yukon and the coldest temperature ever recorded in Canada (-63°C) at Snag, northwest of Kluane Lake, in February 1947.

In 1774, Juan Pérez Hernandez was probably the first European to see the Pacific coast, claiming the area for Spain. Four years later, James Cook – he who had taken Wolfe's fleet up the St. Lawrence in 1750 – was there, too, claiming it for Britain. Only fifteen years after that, in 1793, Northwest Company trader Alexander Mackenzie entered the interior from the other side, over the Rockies via the Peace and upper Fraser rivers, and reaching the Pacific at the mouth of the Bella Coola River. By the middle of the nineteenth century the Union Jack flew firmly over present-day British Columbia, which joined Confederation in 1871 on the promise of a rail link with the east not fulfilled for another fifteen years.

Agents of the Hudson's Bay Company were first on the Yukon scene, in the 1840s – narrowly beating the Russians by sneaking in from Alaska, which only became American (by purchase) in Canada's Confederation year. They were soon followed by missionaries, and then by the Northwest Mounted Police, but it was the great Klondike Gold Rush of 1898 that really opened up the Territory.

Resource-based activities – fishing, forestry and mining – have always been the mainstays of both British Columbian and Yukon economies, increasingly financed by Japanese capital and with much of the produce destined for Pacific Rim and Asian markets. Province and territory encompass 14.5% of Canada. Eastern Canadians have long looked upon British Columbians and Yukoners as "flaky" – but most of them are simply jealous of their western neighbours' more laid back lifestyles.

Above: **Empress Hotel, Victoria.** The traditional cultural expression of lotus-land – afternoon tea in the lobby of the Empress Hotel – beckons across Victoria's intimate little harbour. In 1843 the chief trader at the Hudson's Bay Company's new post on the southern tip of Vancouver Island named it Fort Albert in honour of the young queen's Prince Consort;

but, "Subsequently, a terse message from London compelled the use of Fort Victoria." Head office knew which side its bread was buttered on. And so did Canadian Pacific in 1908 – otherwise true-blue bearers of the white man's burden might have found themselves having tea in the Prince Consort Hotel!

Right: **Thompson River, near Lytton, British Columbia.**

When explorer (and fur trader) Simon Fraser came this way in 1808, he mistakenly believed that his fellow fur trader (and explorer) David Thompson had travelled the river before him; and so he generously named it the Thompson. Thompson returned the compliment by naming a river that Fraser had wrongly concluded to be the Columbia, the Fraser. They were gentlemen in those days.

Both banks of a river once used by both men now carry railway lines, the Canadian Pacific Railway on one bank and the Canadian National Railway on the other – a good indication of the valley's importance in the exploration and development of British Columbia.

*Facing page bottom: **Old City Hall, Victoria**.*

The gold rush of 1858 brought about the creation of British Columbia and lifted Victoria out of the category of Hudson's Bay Company trading post and administrative centre for Vancouver Island and the Queen Charlottes. It became the new colony's capital and was a city by 1862.

When the British Admiralty went ahead with plans for a naval base at nearby Esquimalt, Victoria's future was assured and the city fathers felt free to splurge on a city hall. Despite its relative remoteness, Victoria remained British Columbia's commercial and industrial hub until the 1890s; but after the railway reached Burrard Inlet in 1886, Vancouver soon took its place.

*Right: **Parliament Buildings, Victoria**.*

The city did, however, retain its legislative mantle as the capital of a vastly-expanded British Columbia after 1866. Guess whose statue that is, there on the front lawn?

Above: **Rail Yards, Vancouver.**
The transcontinental railway which began in Halifax ended here. Without much doubt, the most important single artifact in Canadian history has been the steel rail, as in railway line. It was the promise of a rail link with the east that persuaded British Columbia to join the Confederation in 1871, and the need to amortize debts incurred in building railways brought Prince Edward Island and Newfoundland reluctantly onside in 1873 and 1949 respectively. Before the trans-Canada telephone system was organized in the 1930s, the railway was the only physical link between Nova Scotia and British Columbia except Mother Earth herself.

Left: **The "Bay," Vancouver.**
A far cry from the fur-trading post that stood here little more than a century ago, and further still (in both time and distance) from the old Churchill fur post (Fort Prince of Wales) of 1717, this retail megastore stands in the midst of a forest of high-rise office and hotel towers.

Above: **Vancouver Art Gallery.**
Once the Provincial Court House, renovated by renowned architect Arthur Erickson, who also designed such diverse projects as Simon Fraser University, the expanded Bank of Canada building in Ottawa, and the Canadian Embassy in Washington. One wing of the gallery is devoted to the work of Emily Carr – a western, one-woman version of the east's Group of Seven – who died in 1945.

Right: **Sinclair Centre, Vancouver.**
Another recycled structure, the Sinclair Centre was originally the Federal Building housing the Vancouver post office.

Above: **Steam Clock, Gastown, Vancouver.**

On the east side of the Stanley Park peninsula, squeezed inbetween Georgia Street and Burrard Inlet and close to the old Canadian Pacific Railway station, stands the oldest part of Vancouver, and this famous nineteenth-century steam clock. How appropriate that it should stand so close to the old station, for railways and time have always been closely woven.

Left: **Clockwork Clock, Vancouver.**

Too handsome to be a modern design, together with many other public buildings of its generation this thirteen-storey 1911 building is capped with a four-faced clock. Before the coming of the railways, time was a very local affair, set by astronomical conditions and local prejudices. Days began at sunrise and ended at sunset, and the intervening hours were a matter of only local concern.

Railway scheduling required a standardization of time between communities, and in 1884 Canadian Sir Sandford Fleming – a retired railwayman – was instrumental in establishing the international system of time zones that we now take for granted.

Above and left: **Klondike Gold Rush, near Dawson City, Yukon.**
Few people had even heard of the Yukon, fewer still of the Klondike, and virtually none of Rabbit Creek, when prospector George Washington Carmack and his Indian friends, Skookum Jim and Tagish Charlie, dug a shallow shaft there in the summer of 1896. Rabbit Creek was soon renamed Bonanza, and by the following summer half of the civilized world knew about it. Soon every creek along the Klondike and its tributaries was being panned for gold, although the glory days were short-lived. Dredges (which left a wasteland behind them) were more efficient, but their capital costs were enormous. Soon financiers and businessmen rather than "sourdoughs" were the symbols of the Klondike.

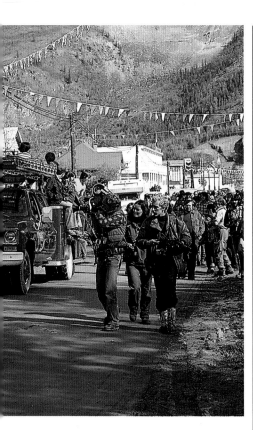

"Discovery Days," Dawson City.
Situated on river flats at the junction of the Yukon and Klondike rivers, Dawson was the inevitable shanty town of the gold rush. In 1896 its population was zero. Two years later, it was a fluctuating 16,000 or 17,000, but from that point on, until the Second World War construction of the Alaska Highway and the beginning of the post-war tourist boom (as fascinating in its way as any gold rush, and, in the long term, probably more profitable), it was something of a ghost town.

This old hardware store (*facing page*) fell into decay, but the opera house (*right*) has been refurbished behind its shabby facade and now plays to capacity crowds of tourists during the festival of "Discovery Days," held each summer.

Above: **Miles Canyon, Whitehorse, Yukon.**

Whitehorse took its name – and the reason for its existence – from the "white horses" of breaking waves in the rapids of Miles Canyon. In '97 and '98, Klondikers paused here, getting ready to raft down the rapids. Now a downstream dam controls the water level; but for many years the rapids were run (both ways) by paddlewheel steamers like the *Klondike II* (*left*) (a replica of the original *Klondike*, wrecked in 1936), which plied the river between Whitehorse and Dawson from 1937 to 1952 but is now dry-docked (and labelled a National Historic Site) at Whitehorse.

Facing page: **Log Cathedral, Whitehorse.**

Constructed in 1900, this Anglican church was used until 1960, serving as the diocesan cathedral when the Diocese was first established. Today the Yukon's capital is a thriving modern community of concrete and glass, bureaucracies being much better than gold rushes in assuring long-term prosperity. There are bigger, if not better, churches in town now, and a new cathedral, but this relic of better days reminds residents of their city's past.

THE OLD LOG
CHURCH
Opened—Oct. 1900

Left and above: **White Pass and Yukon Railway, Yukon.**
A 175-kilometre narrow-gauge railway from (American) tidewater at Skagway, rising over the White Pass at 900 metres and then dropping to Whitehorse, was begun at the height of the gold rush, in 1898, and completed in 1900 – just as the rush was ending! Nevertheless, it carried freight and passengers – in later years, mostly tourists – until 1982. Engine No. 51, built in 1881 and now preserved at Whitehorse, was the first locomotive ever to run north of 60°N. For many years it worked the steepest grades in Canada.

Right and above right: **Alaska Highway, Yukon.**
Initiated by fear of a Japanese invasion of Alaska (they did occupy two islands of the Aleutian chain, stretching far out into the Pacific), the 2,450 km. Alaska Highway, from Dawson Creek in northern British Columbia to Fairbanks, Alaska, was rammed through by American engineers in 1942-43. Since then it has been much improved, but it is still unpaved for most of its length. Opened to the public in 1947, it brought a new industry – tourism – to the Yukon. At Watson Lake, on the British Columbia-Yukon border, a forest of signposts attests to that.

*T*HE NORTHWEST TERRITORIES

*T*he name was originally applied to all those territories of Rupert's Land acquired in 1870 from the Hudson's Bay Company and Great Britain, and whittled away over the years by the formation of Manitoba (1870), the separation of the Yukon (1895), the formation of Saskatchewan and Alberta (1905), and additions to Manitoba (1880 and 1912), and Ontario and Québec (1912). Now reduced to a mere 34% of Canada's area, the Territories' population numbers less than 52,000 – which makes it some of the least populated land on earth – or less than 0.25% of the Canadian total.

Unlike that in any other province (or the only other territory) the majority of the population is aboriginal; and in the whole vast area there are only sixty-four permanent settlements, the largest being the territorial capital of Yellowknife with some 12,000 inhabitants.

Still remote and forbidding, even in the age of air transport, the Territories stretch from Aklavik in the west to Iqaluit (once Frobisher Bay) on Baffin Island, in the east; from Fort Smith and Fort Liard in the south, north to Ellesmere Island's military base at Alert, only 800 kilometres from the Pole and closer to the Soviet Union's Murmansk than to Winnipeg, the nearest Canadian city.

Mineral extraction provides the only economic base, currently mostly mining but with the promise of more oil one day. Because the Territories are so remote, and access is so difficult, tourism plays only a small part in their economy, despite the area's incomparable spectacles, including the Virginia Falls, of the South Nahanni valley in the southwest, and the rugged vistas of Auyuittuq – our only national park above the Arctic Circle – on Baffin Island in the west.

Below: **Mission Church, Fort Providence.**

For once, the Hudson's Bay Company – whose initials, it has been claimed, really stand for 'Here Before Christ' – failed to live up to its reputation. Christ, in the guise of Roman Catholic missionary Father Grolier, established a mission here in the 1850s, and a Grey Nuns boarding school for Indian children followed in 1867. The Bay was a poor third on the scene.

Right: **Halfway House, Fort Fitzgerald.**

Once it was Salt River House, a Hudson's Bay post on the Slave River situated at the head of a set of major rapids. Then, it was a way-station on the old voyageur route between Lake Athabaska and Great Slave Lake which, in turn, linked the Hudson's Bay watershed with the Mackenzie River basin; but wilderness roads now carry goods more easily and economically and Fort Fitzgerald flourishes no more.

Left and below: **Gold Mine, Yellowknife.**

Gold was found in the vicinity of Yellowknife from the turn of the century, but panning placer gold is a chancy business, soon washed out. Unlike the Klondike case, however, at Yellowknife a mother lode was located in 1944, and is still worked by conventional hard-rock mining techniques. The prosperity two gold mines have brought was supplemented by Yellowknife's selection as the territorial capital in 1967.

Facing page bottom: **Wildcat Café, Yellowknife.**

A local symbol, this log-built one-time house of doubtful repute remains one of the oldest, if not the oldest, buildings in Yellowknife. Nowadays it is open only in summer to serve food and drink, and is staffed by ladies of very good repute.

Above: **Wardair Monument, Yellowknife.**

"Bush flying" conjures up the romantic image of small planes bringing patients to medical care, delivering supplies to prospectors or trappers on the shores of lonely lakes, and carrying missionaries, policemen, and the like, about their northern business. All that was (and is) true, but the other – economically more important – side of the coin was the movement of heavy freight – mining equipment – needed to develop the roadless north's resource potential.

The Bristol Freighter could carry some 8,000 kilogrammes of freight, including, on occasion, bulldozers and rock-crushers. In 1946, Max Ward established a charter business in Yellowknife to serve the mining community. His first attempt failed, but in 1953 he founded Wardair and in 1957 added two Bristol Freighters to his growing fleet. This one, as well as servicing industry, became the first wheeled aircraft – as opposed to the sort with skis – to land at the North Pole. Now it rests permanently on another kind of pole, a memorial to the entrepreneurial bush flyers who really opened up the north.

VIMY RIDGE

REMEMBER · N'OUBLIONS PAS

Above: ***Vimy Memorial, France.***
On Easter Monday, 1917, 60,000 Canadians, from every part of the Dominion, rose from their trenches and stormed Vimy Ridge in one of the First World War's most successful battles, and one which established Canada's place and reputation in a wider world. After the war, France gave the battlefield to Canada and Ottawa financed this dramatic monument to the memory of the 3,600 men who perished in taking it.

Men who were there, and afterwards rose high in civilian life, have argued that Canada truly became a nation on Vimy Ridge. Before the First World War, few Nova Scotians knew anything of Manitoba, Québeckers nothing of British Columbia, and even the thought of Alberta was anathema to New Brunswickers while few Saskatchewanis had even heard of Prince Edward Island. Despite the railways, the country was too vast, travel too difficult, and there was neither radio nor television to disseminate information.

The Canadian Expeditionary Force had brought young men together from every part of Canada and every walk of life. They had learned more about each other in the crucible of war – their strengths and weaknesses, likes and dislikes, habits and motives and caprices – than their fathers could have imagined. What was still needed was some great achievement in common to solidify the comradeship of the trenches. It came on Easter Monday, 1917.